CH

yes

POW

Little People, BIG DREAMS
MUHAMMAD ALI

Written by
Mª Isabel Sánchez Vegara

Illustrated by
Brosmind

Frances Lincoln
Children's Books

Once, there was a little boy from Kentucky who knew he would go far in life.

His name was Cassius, and he lived in a little house with his parents and younger brother.

One day, someone stole his brand-new bicycle. He told the police officer that he wanted to face the thief. The officer said: "Cassius...you better learn how to fight first."

Soon, Cassius was learning how to box.
He was not the strongest fighter, but he
had a secret weapon: he was
faster than anyone else.

POW

Fight after fight, Cassius proved himself as a junior boxer. His talent took him to the Olympics in Rome, where he won a gold medal. But it was not enough! He dreamed of going professional.

He trained harder than ever, and not just in the ring. Cassius set his sights on the world heavyweight championship.

To tease his opponents, Cassius often used rhymes, describing how he was going to win.

...AND STING
LIKE A BEE.

Some thought it was trash talk, but
it sounded like poetry...and it worked!

He got his chance to fight for the title against
Sonny Liston, one of the world's toughest fighters.

Everyone thought Cassius was scared to death,
but he proved the champion's belt belonged to him.

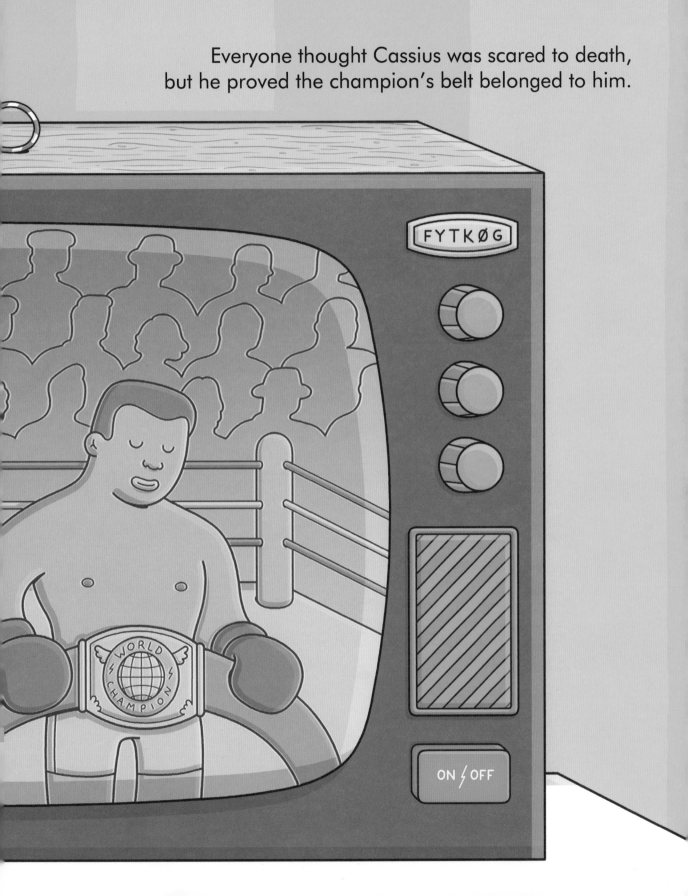

Cassius was not just a famous boxer, but a courageous defender of African American rights, in a time when it was dangerous to speak up.

He also became inspired by the teachings of Islam and changed his name to Muhammad Ali, a beautiful Arabic name that made him feel strong and proud to be himself.

Then a war started on the other side of the world. Ali thought it was wrong and refused to fight in it. He was stripped of his title and banned from boxing for three years.

But for him, beliefs were more important.

When Ali came back, he did it as only the greatest do! The Ali shuffle, the rope-a-dope...he won some of his most famous fights, becoming the first boxer to win the heavyweight belt three times.

Ali was admired and loved by people from all around the world. And when he retired, he gave all that love back, by working for charities and helping others.

Since then, many young boxers have followed in the steps of Muhammad Ali—the little boy who used to say: "One day, I'm going to be the greatest."

MUHAMMAD ALI

(Born 1942 • Died 2016)

1954   1962

Cassius Marcellus Clay Jr. was born and raised in Louisville, Kentucky. When Cassius was 12 years old, someone stole his bicycle. The police officer on duty suggested he should come to his boxing class and learn how to fight. Cassius started to train as an amateur boxer and won 100 out of his 105 fights. He hated training, but knew if he worked hard he would become a champion. At age 18, he made it to the 1960 Summer Olympics in Rome, bringing home a gold medal in the light heavyweight division. This was enough for Cassius to turn his dream of boxing into a career. He went professional, and at 22, he won his first heavyweight title against favorite-to-win Sonny Liston. From then on, Cassius was a formidable fighter. He was fast, smart, and used slick rhymes to taunt his

1965

1966

opponents. Cassius later converted to the Muslim faith and changed his name to Muhammad Ali. When the Vietnam War started, Ali refused to fight because he felt it was unjust. He was banned from boxing for three years. When he returned to the ring, he won three more heavyweight titles. But Ali was more than just a boxer. He spoke out about civil rights and racial discrimination, and gave love and hope to his community. In later years, Ali suffered from Parkinson's disease. Despite his illness, he continued to spread hope by raising money for charities that helped people with the disease. Today, Muhammad Ali is remembered as the greatest boxer of all time, and a champion who lived by his words: "Don't count the days, make the days count."

Want to find out more about **Muhammad Ali?**
Read one of these great books:

Young, Gifted and Black by Jamia Wilson and Andrea Pippins

Who Was Muhammad Ali? by James Buckley Jr. and Stephen Marchesi

Muhammad Ali: A Champion Is Born by Gene Barretta and Frank Morrison

If you're in Louisville, Kentucky, you could even visit the Ali Center to learn more about Muhammad's life and principles.

BOARD BOOKS

COCO CHANEL

ISBN: 978-1-78603-245-4

MAYA ANGELOU

ISBN: 978-1-78603-249-2

FRIDA KAHLO

ISBN: 978-1-78603-247-8

AMELIA EARHART

ISBN: 978-1-78603-252-2

MARIE CURIE

ISBN: 978-1-78603-253-9

ADA LOVELACE

ISBN:978-1-78603-259-1

ROSA PARKS

ISBN: 978-1-78603-263-8

EMMELINE PANKHURST

ISBN: 978-1-78603-261-4

AUDREY HEPBURN

ISBN: 978-1-78603-255-3

ELLA FITZGERALD

ISBN:978-1-78603-257-7

BOOKS & PAPER DOLLS

EMMELINE PANKHURST

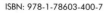
ISBN: 978-1-78603-400-7

MARIE CURIE

ISBN: 978-1-78603-401-4

BOX SETS

WOMEN IN ART

ISBN: 978-1-78603-428-1

WOMEN IN SCIENCE

ISBN: 978-1-78603-429-8

Collect the *Little People,* **BIG DREAMS** series:

FRIDA KAHLO

ISBN: 978-1-84780-783-0

COCO CHANEL

ISBN: 978-1-84780-784-7

MAYA ANGELOU

ISBN: 978-1-84780-889-9

AMELIA EARHART

ISBN: 978-1-84780-888-2

AGATHA CHRISTIE

ISBN: 978-1-84780-960-5

MARIE CURIE

ISBN: 978-1-84780-962-9

ROSA PARKS
ISBN: 978-1-78603-018-4

AUDREY HEPBURN

ISBN: 978-1-78603-053-5

EMMELINE PANKHURST

ISBN: 978-1-78603-020-7

ELLA FITZGERALD

ISBN: 978-1-78603-087-0

ADA LOVELACE

ISBN: 978-1-78603-076-4

JANE AUSTEN

ISBN: 978-1-78603-120-4

GEORGIA O'KEEFFE

ISBN: 978-1-78603-122-8

HARRIET TUBMAN
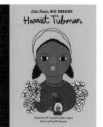
ISBN: 978-1-78603-227-0

ANNE FRANK

ISBN: 978-1-78603-229-4

MOTHER TERESA

ISBN: 978-1-78603-230-0

JOSEPHINE BAKER

ISBN: 978-1-78603-228-7

L. M. MONTGOMERY

ISBN: 978-1-78603-233-1

JANE GOODALL

ISBN: 978-1-78603-231-7

SIMONE DE BEAUVOIR
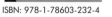
ISBN: 978-1-78603-232-4

MUHAMMAD ALI

ISBN: 978-1-78603-331-4

STEPHEN HAWKING

ISBN: 978-1-78603-333-8

Brimming with creative inspiration, how-to projects, and useful information to enrich your everyday life, Quarto Knows is a favorite destination for those pursuing their interests and passions. Visit our site and dig deeper with our books into your area of interest: Quarto Creates, Quarto Cooks, Quarto Homes, Quarto Lives, Quarto Drives, Quarto Explores, Quarto Gifts, or Quarto Kids.

First Published in the US in 2019 by Frances Lincoln Children's Books, an imprint of The Quarto Group.

400 First Avenue North, Suite 400, Minneapolis, MN 55401, USA.

T (612) 344-8100 F (612) 344-8692 **www.QuartoKnows.com**

First Published in Spain in 2019 under the title Pequeña & Grande Muhammad Ali

by Alba Editorial, s.l.u., Baixada de Sant Miquel, 1, 08002 Barcelona

www.albaeditorial.es

ISBN 978-1-78603-331-4

The illustrations were created with digital techniques.

Set in Futura BT.

Published by Rachel Williams • Designed by Karissa Santos

Edited by Katy Flint • Production by Jenny Cundill

Manufactured in Guangdong, China CC112018

9 7 5 3 1 2 4 6 8

Photographic acknowledgments (pages 28–29, from left to right) 1. 12-year-old Cassius Clay, 1954 © Bettmann via Getty Images 2. Cassius Clay vs. Archie Moore, 1962 © The Stanley Weston Archive via Getty Images 3. Muhammad Ali meets fans in London, 1966 © Hulton Archive via Getty Images 4. Muhammad Ali taunting Sonny Liston, 1965 © Bettmann via Getty Images